MARVEL STUDIOS

Piano / Vocal / Guitar

WandaVision

Music from the Disney+ Original Series

ISBN 978-1-70513-861-8

Images and Artwork © 2021 MARVEL

Visit Hal Leonard Online at
www.halleonard.com

Contact us:
Hal Leonard
7777 West Bluemound Road
Milwaukee, WI 53213
Email: info@halleonard.com

In Europe, contact:
Hal Leonard Europe Limited
42 Wigmore Street
Marylebone, London, W1U 2RN
Email: info@halleonardeurope.com

In Australia, contact:
Hal Leonard Australia Pty. Ltd.
4 Lentara Court
Cheltenham, Victoria, 3192 Australia
Email: info@halleonard.com.au

A NEWLYWED COUPLE

Music and Lyrics by KRISTEN ANDERSON-LOPEZ
and ROBERT LOPEZ

Oh,   a

new-ly-wed cou - ple just moved to town, a reg-u-lar hus - band and

wife   who left the big cit - y   to find a qui - et

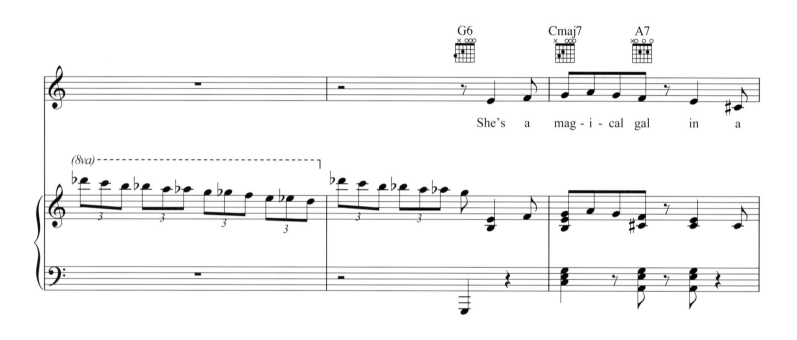

WANDAVISION!

Music and Lyrics by KRISTEN ANDERSON-LOPEZ
and ROBERT LOPEZ

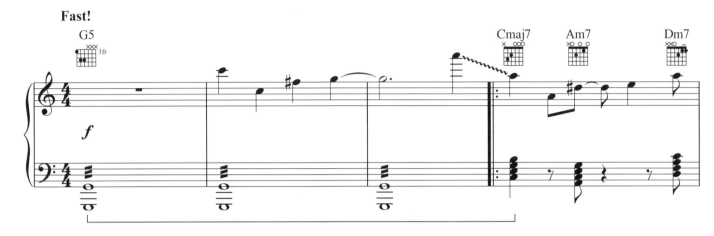

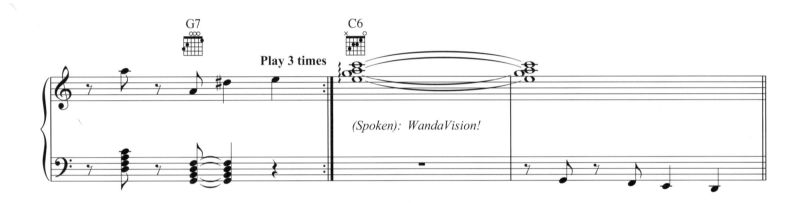

(Spoken): WandaVision!

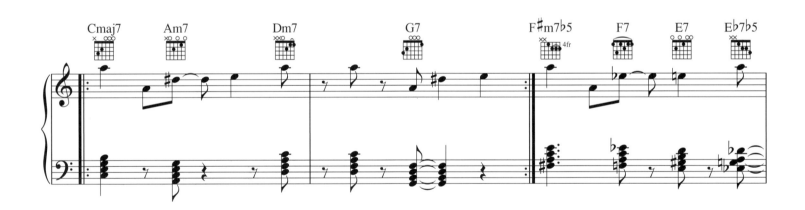

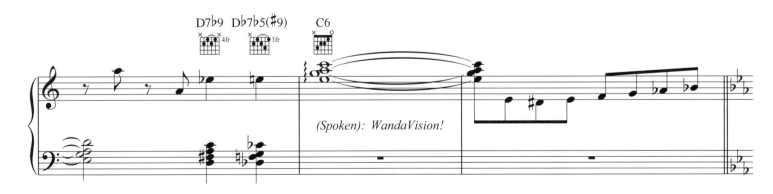

(Spoken): WandaVision!

WE GOT SOMETHING COOKING

Music and Lyrics by KRISTEN ANDERSON-LOPEZ
and ROBERT LOPEZ

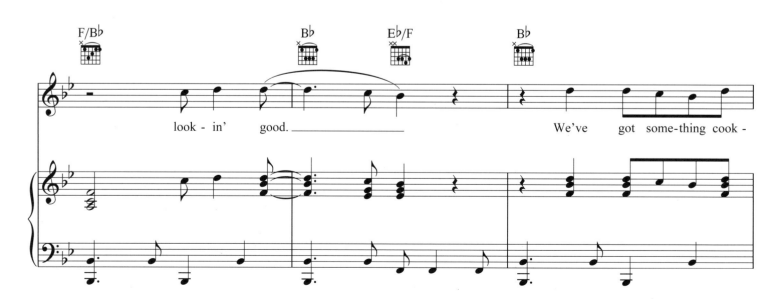

MAKING IT UP AS WE GO ALONG

Music and Lyrics by KRISTEN ANDERSON-LOPEZ
and ROBERT LOPEZ

Moderate '80s Soft Rock

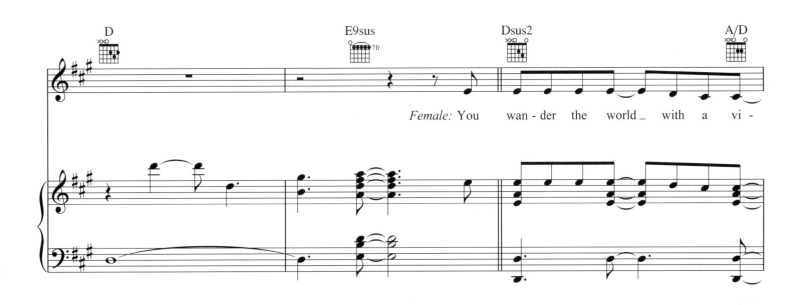

Female: You wan-der the world_ with a vi-

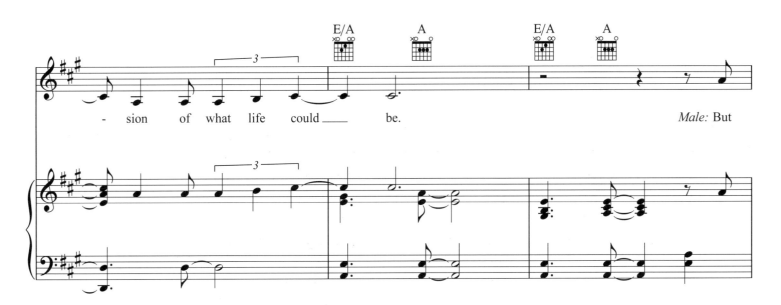

-sion of what life could ___ be.

Male: But

LET'S KEEP IT GOING

Music and Lyrics by KRISTEN ANDERSON-LOPEZ
and ROBERT LOPEZ

Early 2000s Punk Rock

Wan - da! Wan - da - Vi - sion!

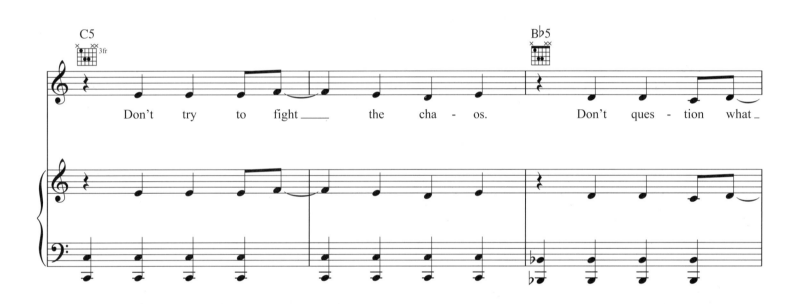

Don't try to fight _____ the cha - os. Don't ques - tion what _____

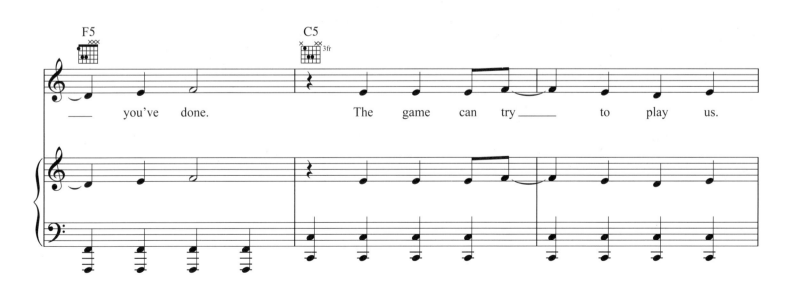

_____ you've done. The game can try _____ to play us.

AGATHA ALL ALONG

Music and Lyrics by KRISTEN ANDERSON-LOPEZ
and ROBERT LOPEZ

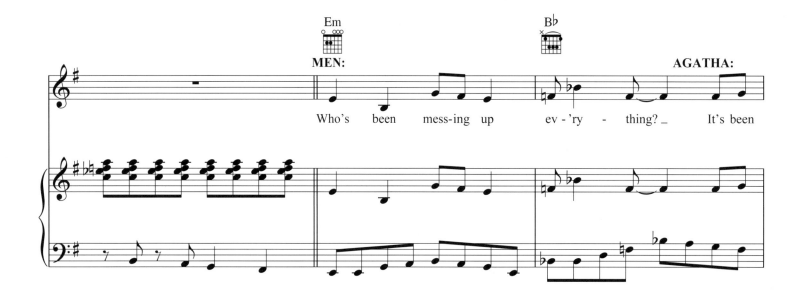

MEN: Who's been mess-ing up ev-'ry-thing?__ It's been

A-ga-tha all a-long.

W-V 2000

Music and Lyrics by KRISTEN ANDERSON-LOPEZ
and ROBERT LOPEZ

2000s TV theme

WANDA'S THEME
(End Credits from *WandaVision*)

By CHRISTOPHE BECK